Wolfgang Ecke
The Secret of the Chinese Junk

Wolfgang Ecke (1927–1983)

Sein Name ist zu einem Begriff für gute, spannende Unterhaltung geworden. Seine Bücher beziehen ihre Spannung aus der Aufforderung zum Mitdenken, durch lebendige, oft humorvolle Dialoge – und nicht durch sensationelle Gewalt. Wolfgang Ecke sagte selbst: »Ich behaupte, es gibt keinen Kinder-Krimi! Es gibt nur Kriminalgeschichten, die als Lektüre für Kinder geeignet sind; wobei es unbedeutend ist, ob sie eigens für Kinder geschrieben wurden.«

Er hat über 600 Hörspiele geschrieben, von denen unzählige, ebenso wie ein Großteil seiner über fünfzig Bücher, in viele Sprachen übersetzt wurden. Er war ständiger Mitarbeiter bei zahlreichen in- und ausländischen Radiosendern, schrieb für Jugendzeitschriften, produzierte Platten und auch einige Fernsehfilme. In den Ravensburger Taschenbüchern sind neben mehreren Einzeltiteln folgende Serien von ihm erschienen:

Wer knackt die Nuß?
Perry Clifton
Club der Detektive (auch auf englisch)
Meisterdetektiv Balduin Pfiff

Für mehr als fünf Millionen verkaufte Ravensburger Taschenbücher erhielt Ecke fünfmal das »Goldene Taschenbuch«.

Wolfgang Ecke selbst über sein Leben:

»Geboren dort, wo Karl May starb: in Radebeul, und zwar am 24. November 1927. Schulbesuch, da Pflicht. ›Sehr gut‹ in Deutsch und Geographie. Alle übrigen Zensuren nicht überlieferungswürdig. Mit 13 Jahren in ein militärisches Internat. Außer Marschieren und Strammstehen auch Klavier, Schlagzeug und Fagott gelernt. Gelungener Versuch, den Krieg unbeschadet zu überleben. Danach Hochschule für Musik und Theater in Dresden. Bereits 1946 aus politischen Gründen von der Hochschule relegiert.«
Zwischen 1945 und 1952 lebte Ecke »abwechselnd überall und in Dresden«. Anfang der 70er Jahre ließ er sich mit seiner Frau und seinen beiden Töchtern (und zwei afghanischen Windhunden und zahlreichen Katzen) im bayerischen Alpenvorland nieder; zuletzt wohnte er oberhalb des Staffelsees in Murnau.

Wolfgang Ecke

The Secret of the Chinese Junk

and other detective stories

Illustrations
by Rolf Rettich

Otto Maier Ravensburg

Hinweis

Schwierige Vokabeln werden nur beim ersten Auftreten in den Fußnoten unten auf der Seite aufgeführt, ansonsten im alphabetischen Gesamtverzeichnis. Andere Vokabeln sind nur im alphabetischen Gesamtverzeichnis am Schluß des Buches zu finden. Es empfiehlt sich also, häufiger dort nachzuschlagen.

Als Ravensburger Taschenbuch Band 648
erschienen 1980

Die Geschichten erschienen 1972, 1973, 1974
als deutsche Originalausgabe in folgenden
Ravensburger Taschenbüchern:
RTB 227 Solo für Melodica
RTB 264 Das Geheimnis der alten Dschunke
RTB 306 Das Haus der 99 Geister

Die englische Erstausgabe erschien bei
Methuen Children's Books Ltd., London unter dem Titel
„Be A Super Sleuth with the Case of the Stolen Paintings"

Aus dem Deutschen von Stella und Vernon Humphries
Bearbeitung: Uwe Lüer

Umschlagkonzeption: Graphisches Atelier Otto Maier Verlag
Umschlagbild: Walter Emmrich, unter Verwendung
einer Zeichnung von Rolf Rettich

Gesamtherstellung: Ebner Ulm
Printed in Germany

13 12 11 10 9 98 97 96 95 94

ISBN 3-473-38648-0

Contents

Solutions: *easy
**quite difficult
***difficult

1 The case of the stolen paintings

At 2.20 a.m. the thieves left the art gallery unseen.
At half-past two, however, the night-watchman discovered the theft and called the police.
At 3 a.m., roadblocks were set up at all the main roads, while airports and railway stations were also informed. Nevertheless, when the 5 a.m. radio news first mentioned the robbery of two valuable paintings, the thieves were already more than a hundred miles from the scene of the crime. While Carl Pasoli watched the traffic behind them, Pierre Auger concentrated on his driving, making certain he wasn't going too fast. He knew of many robberies that had come to grief because the driver had been stopped for speeding.
His accomplice however had no patience with such caution.
"For Heaven's sake put your foot down, Pierre!" he told him.
"I'm going fast enough already," replied Auger calmly.
"But every old car on the road is overtaking us!"
Pierre nodded and glanced at the speedometer again. And when, a short time later, he saw that a big truck was trying to get by, he pulled over to the left and allowed it to overtake.

---

roadblock	–	Straßensperre
to come to grief	–	hier: unglücklich enden
to speed	–	(zu) schnell fahren
accomplice	–	Komplize
caution	–	Vorsicht

"We'll never get there if you drive so slowly", Pasoli went on nagging. Then for the umpteenth time he turned to the two precious Old Masters and tucked the blankets round them more securely.
"I'll bet there isn't another car on the road at this moment with a load worth more than ours," said Pierre.
"And I'll bet there isn't another one crawling so slowly

---

to nag – meckern, nörgeln
for the umpteenth time – zum x-ten Mal
to tuck – ziehen

– unless they've something wrong with the engine!" replied Carl.
The man at the steering-wheel smiled. "You've still a lot to learn, Carl – that is, if you want to get on in this line of business. A craftsman may have to serve an apprenticeship, and after three or four years, he's qualified. But a good thief never stops learning. And until you understand that, you'll never be any good."
For a while Carl Pasoli was silent. Then he said: "I sometimes wonder why you never went in for teaching! You'd be good at it. Why didn't you?"
Just then Pierre glanced in the mirror once again and this time he started. Police! He was about to accelerate wildly, but he thought better of it. That would have been a stupid thing to do.
A few moments later it was all over. Pierre Auger and Carl Pasoli were on their way back to where they had started from with an escort of three police officers. And under custody, inside a police car. And neither of them ever found out which mistake they had made.

As a matter of fact, we don't know, either, why the police stopped, and then searched, their car. Nor do we need to know. What we have to find out is this: in which European country did the art theft take place?

---

craftsman	– Handwerker
qualified	– qualifiziert, ausgebildet
to go in for	– s. befassen mit, begeistern für
to start	– hier: zusammenfahren, erschrecken
to accelerate	– beschleunigen
under custody	– unter Bewachung

2 Bring on the clowns!

The Hermann Hoff Circus had already been in town for four days. It had been a great success. On the first three days every seat had been sold, and there was a large audience in the Big Top on the fourth night.
It was about a quarter to ten that evening when Hermann Hoff, the owner and ring-master, left his caravan. As usual, he went to see that his favourite white horse Tarantella was ready and harnessed for his big act. The dainty Spanish tight-rope walker, Olivia Franto, had already begun her daring and fascinating act on the high-wire.
Joe Wilsing, the animal trainer, who was sitting on the steps of his caravan, saw the ring-master vanish in the direction of the animal compound.
A few moments later, he also saw the clown, who was just disappearing into Mr Hoff's caravan. However, Joe Wilsing thought nothing of it. He got up and went to see to the lions.
Hermann Hoff returned to his caravan at half-past ten, and was horrified. Someone had broken into the cupboard where he kept the money. The whole of the box-

---

Big Top	– gr. Zirkuszelt
ring master	– Zirkusdirektor
to harness	– zäumen
dainty	– zierlich
tight-rope walker	– Seiltänzer(in)
daring	– wagemutig
vanish	– verschwinden
compound	– Platz, Gehege
horrified	– entsetzt

office takings had gone, as well as the cash he always kept in reserve. "Don't lose your head," he told himself, and realizing that the thief might have left some fingerprints he picked up the telephone cautiously.

When Detective-Sergeant Watzmann arrived fifteen minutes later, accompanied by two of his men, Mr Hoff suddenly remembered seeing Joe Wilsing earlier that evening. And Joe, in turn, remembered seeing the clown. There seemed to be no doubt at all as to who was the thief. But there was an unexpected difficulty: there were three clowns in the circus. They called themselves The Three Patonis, and they not only worked together but wore the same costume and the same make-up and they shared a caravan.

Detective-Sergeant Watzmann knew how to deal with the situation. He ordered the ring-master and the animal trainer to keep quiet about the incident, and not to mention it to anyone at all until he gave them permission. So even at midnight no one else in the circus had been told about the theft.

As the police officer approached the clowns' caravan, it was ten minutes past midnight, and he could hear angry voices inside. He knocked at the door and entered. Three pairs of eyes stared at him, half curiously, half suspiciously.

"Detective-Sergeant Watzmann!" he announced crisply. "May I come in?" Without waiting for an answer, he

---

box-office takings	– Kasseneinnahmen
cash	– Klein-, Wechselgeld
in turn	– seinerseits, wiederum
to share	– teilen, gemeinsam benutzen
incident	– Vorfall
suspicious(ly)	– argwöhnisch
crisp(ly)	– forsch

made his way inside the caravan and closed the door behind him.

"You are Pierre Cobin, Max Lanscher and Bill Hempell, I believe."

The clowns, who had removed their costumes by now, nodded, still surprised.

"What is it you want?" asked Pierre, while Hempell looked daggers at Lanscher and muttered: "I expect Max has been up to his tricks again!"

It seemed as if the previous quarrel would break out again, but the sergeant firmly intervened. "There was a robbery here tonight and we know for certain that one of you must be the culprit. We have an eye-witness."

"It wasn't me," stated Pierre Cobin, unruffled. "And you can't prove anything against me."

"But you're up to your neck in debt!" hissed Hempell.

"That's right," Max agreed. "He's always borrowing money, and he never pays it back."

"You'd better keep your mouth shut, Max," Cobin protested, "or the sergeant will crack your alibi."

"And then he'll find out that you've been prowling round the ring-master's caravan ever since we arrived," Hempell went on.

---

to look daggers at	– mit Blicken durchbohren
to be up to tricks	– Streiche spielen
previous	– vorherig(e)
quarrel	– Streit
firm(ly)	– fest, entschieden
to intervene	– dazwischentreten, -fahren
culprit	– Schuldige(r)
eye-witness	– Augenzeuge
unruffled	– unerschüttert, gelassen
in debt	– verschuldet
to hiss	– zischen
to crack	– knacken, als falsch beweisen
to prowl	– schleichen, sich herumtreiben

"You're a liar!" shouted Lanscher, making a lunge for Hempell.
The sergeant separated the two men. "Where were you between the high-wire act and Mr Hoff's performance, Mr Lanscher?" he enquired.
"In the canteen," answered Lanscher gruffly. "Why don't you ask Cobin where he was?"
"Well, Mr Cobin?" said the officer. "Where were you at the time?"
"Here in the caravan."
"And you?"
Bill Hempell made a vague gesture. "I'm pretty certain I was by the entrance to the animal compound."
Pierre Cobin tapped Watzmann on the arm. "Why don't you produce your eye-witness, Sergeant? That'd be the simplest way, wouldn't it?"
"I bet there isn't any witness," sneered Lanscher. "It's all bluff..."
"I agree," nodded Bill Hempell emphatically. "And even if there were a witness, it doesn't mean much. Anyone can dress up as a clown, after all."
Detective-Sergeant Watzmann smiled and opened the door. His two officers entered immediately. "We'll be taking *him* for a start", said the sergeant, pointing to one of the three. "I'll be very surprised if he hasn't something to do with the case."

Which of the three men did the sergeant mean?

---

to make a lunge for – losstürzen auf
gruff(ly) – mürrisch, grob
to produce – (hervor-)holen
to sneer – feixen, grinsen
for a start – zunächst einmal

3 The squatters who got a fright

There were just the two of them, sitting in a corner of the dreary little pub, which at that early hour was otherwise empty. No one disturbed the sinister conversation of the two layabouts.
"How do you fancy a few days' holiday?" enquired Sid.
"A holiday?" grinned Wally. "Are you treating me?"
Sid shook his head. "I've got it all worked out. Do you know Beechwood Hills?"
"Sure: the new estate where all the posh bungalows are."
"Right first time. I've just found out that one of them is unoccupied at present. The family's gone skiing in Switzerland until the end of the month."
"So what?"
"It's just the place to get away from it all for a week or so. Food, whisky and cigars all supplied free."
Wally looked doubtful. "In a cold house, where it would not be safe to switch on the light, even? Not very cosy, I'd say," he objected.

---

to disturb	– stören
sinister	– böse, schlimm
layabout	– Gammler
how do you fancy…	– wie würden dir… gefallen?
to treat	– zum Narren halten
estate	– Siedlung
posh	– piekfein
unoccupied	– unbewohnt
at present	– gegenwärtig
supplied	– vorrätig, vorhanden
cosy	– gemütlich
to object	– einwenden

His friend dismissed such objections with a wave of his hand. "First of all a classy joint like that has central heating, and secondly the window blinds are down everywhere. We can switch on all the lights for as long as we like. You can't see a glimmer from the outside."

Two days later, on 8 January, with the thermometer standing at −5°C, Sid and Wally put into action their "Operation Beechwood Hills Holiday".

Towards midnight they tiptoed up to the house, and Sid, who was an expert at picking locks, opened the front door in less than sixty seconds.

A pleasant warmth greeted them, and Wally kicked off his shoes as soon as he saw that there were thick carpets everywhere. But when he realized that the fridge was full of food, and the freezer was crammed to bursting, he grew really excited. He quickly took a couple of plump ducks out of the freezer and left them to thaw on the kitchen table.

Eighteen hours went by.

Sid had put a match to the huge log fire, and soon it was blazing cheerfully. Wally set the table, for the ducks were brown by now and roasted to a turn. Then they switched on the television, carefully keeping the volume down.

---

to dismiss	– hier: vom Tisch fegen
classy joint	– ‚klasse Bude'
to put into action	– wahr machen
to tiptoe	– auf Zehenspitzen gehen
to pick locks	– Schlösser knacken
freezer	– Tiefkühlfach
crammed to bursting	– rammelvoll, zum Bersten voll
plump	– mollig, fett
to thaw	– tauen
log fire	– Kaminfeuer
to blaze	– glühen, brennen
volume	– Lautstärke

They were busily devouring the delicious legs of duck and smacking their lips with enjoyment when the weatherman appeared on the screen, forecasting that the cold weather would go on for some time. But before the two uninvited guests had had the chance to discuss this prospect, there was a ring at the door-bell.
Wally was so frightened that he didn't know what to do first: should he swallow the meat in his mouth, or should he creep away into the nearest cupboard? For several moments they both sat as frozen as statues. By the time their minds began to function again, it was too late.
The crews of two police patrol-cars stood in the middle of the room, and clapped on two pairs of handcuffs.
A remark they made later showed that even after sentence the two "holidaymakers" hadn't found out what was the mistake that had led to the police discovering them.

And do you know, Super Sleuths? Here's a hint: their mistake had nothing to do with the lights, the television – or the ducks.

---

to devour	– verschlingen
to smack	– lecken
to forecast	– vorhersagen, ankündigen
prospect	– Aussicht, Vorschau
handcuffs	– Handschellen
sentence	– Urteil
sleuth	– Detektiv
hint	– Hinweis, Hilfe

4 The secret of the Chinese junk

Suddenly, there she was, as if she had stolen into port at dead of night. Broad, shallow, mysterious, she rocked gently from one side to the other at the quay of Ostend. The admiring Belgian harbour-workers stared at her inquisitively. They couldn't remember ever having seen an authentic Chinese junk in Ostend before.
Soon the most fantastic rumours about this ship from the Far East were circulating round the Belgian town.

When Inspector Jan van Helder walked into his office that morning, his colleague, Tony Himst, immediately told him the news. "Have you heard what's been happening at the harbour?"
"No, nothing. Has it run dry?"
Tony Himst laughed. "No, nothing like that. But we have a visitor from the Far East. A Chinese junk has tied up here."

---

junk	– Dschunke
Chinese	– chinesisch; Chinese(n)
stolen into port at dead of night	– um Mitternacht heimlich in den Hafen geschlichen
shallow	– flach, ohne Tiefgang
to rock	– schaukeln
quay	– Kai
inquisitively	– fragend, neugierig
authentic	– echt
rumour	– Gerücht
to circulate	– in Umlauf sein
to run dry	– austrocknen

The inspector was genuinely surprised. "A junk, eh? Where's she registered?"
"I've no idea," answered Himst. "All I know is that she's as old as the hills, and her name is *Su Lin Fu.*"
"And there are Chinese swarming all over the place, I suppose," said the inspector smiling.
They discussed the junk's possible route for a few minutes, and then the more important everyday business of police headquarters demanded their attention.
Exactly an hour later, however, two things happened, and they were of such importance that the very building seemed to be crackling with excitement. At 9.10 a.m. there was first a report from an agent that Jacko Barnelli had been seen in Ostend. Unfortunately, the agent could not give more precise details, because at the time of his discovery the agent happened to be riding in a bus while Barnelli overtook it in a car.
Although his tip was of that sort that every other policeman in Belgium would have jumped from his chair, Inspector van Helder remained calm and unmoved, for he doubted very much that the report was reliable. What would one of Europe's best known jewel-thieves be doing in Ostend of all places? What could he possibly

---

to register	– anmelden, registrieren
headquarters	– Zentrale
to demand	– in Anspruch nehmen, fordern
to crackle with excitement	– vor Erregung knistern
unfortunately	– unglücklicherweise
precise	– genau
happened to be riding	– fuhr zufällig
to overtake	– überholen
calm	– ruhig
to doubt	– bezweifeln
reliable	– verläßlich
...of all places	– ausgerechnet in...

want there? Probably it was only one more of Barnelli's many red herrings to put Interpol on the wrong track. There were big rewards offered for his capture in seven countries – more than £ 10,000 in all. On the other hand, in the last three years he had made at least fifty robberies. And since Jacko worked alone, and knew how to alter his appearance like a chameleon, the task of the police was anything but easy.

His latest and much-admired coup had been to walk into the shop of one of the biggest jewellers in Antwerp dressed as a monk. He pretended to be embarassed, and waited humbly in the background until most of the customers had left the elegant shop.

What happened next was like something in a thriller on the stage. All at once, the monk pulled a gas-mask over his face, which had been completely hidden by his cowl, and threw on the floor seven little glass phials filled with a liquid, and within fifteen seconds customers and staff had all collapsed, unconscious. The "monk" locked both doors and began to collect the most beautiful and valuable of the precious stones and pieces of jewellery. All

---

red herring	– Ablenkungsmanöver
the wrong track	– die falsche Fährte
to alter	– ändern
appearance	– Erscheinung
task	– Aufgabe
monk	– Mönch
to pretend	– vortäuschen
embarrassed	– verwirrt, verlegen
humbly	– demütig, ergeben
cowl	– Kutte
phial	– Fläschchen
liquid	– Flüssigkeit
staff	– Belegschaft
unconscious	– bewußtlos
valuable	– wertvoll
precious stone	– Edelstein

that the police found afterwards was the monk's cowl. Inspector van Helder remembered all these details. All the same, he did not draw any hasty conclusions on hear-

---

conclusion – Schlußfolgerung

ing the agent's report. But then, at 10 o'clock, there came a telex from Interpol headquarters in Paris that seemed to make Helder really jump up, for now Barnelli's story suddenly acquired enormous importance. The telex read:

ALEXIS GALANOS THE GREEK SUSPECTED OF BEING RECEIVER OF STOLEN GOODS ON INTERNATIONAL SCALE LEFT RAMSGATE ENGLAND ON NIGHT OF 28 ABOARD CHARTERED JUNK SU LIN FU. TOOK SOUTH-EAST COURSE. ALL STATIONS ON NORTH-WEST COAST OF FRANCE BELGIUM NETHERLANDS ARE ASKED TO KEEP SPECIAL LOOK-OUT.

"So the Barnelli report must be right!" exclaimed Tony Himst. Van Helder nodded absentmindedly. For several minutes, all one could hear was the ticking of the old clock. The inspector gave his instructions. "At first sight," he began, "it looks as if there must be a direct connection between the appearance of the Chinese junk and Barnelli's coming here. On the one hand a notorious 'fence', and on the other a well-known thief... But the telex says Galanos is only suspected of receiving stolen goods, so his guilt has never been proved. It's perfectly possible that he's here on a harmless pleasure-cruise and nothing else. In that case, Tony, find out from whom he chartered the junk, what's her crew, and how long she

---

to acquire	– gewinnen
telex	– Fernschreiben
the Greek suspected...	– der Grieche, der in Verdacht steht...
scale	– Ebene
to keep look-out	– Obacht geben, aufpassen
absentmindedly	– geistesabwesend
fence	– Hehler, Verkäufer von gestohlenen Waren
guilt	– Schuld
to prove	– beweisen
cruise	– (See-)Reise, Vergnügungsfahrt

wants to stay here. And I'll make sure that not even a mouse can leave the boat or go on board unseen."

About two hours later, the two police officers met again. Tony Himst reported first. "Well, I've found out quite a lot."

"Good. Fire away!"

"First about the junk. *Su Lin Fu* is registered in Ramsgate, England, which is where her owner lives too. His name is Sir Keith Foreman. He's a man of seventy, who describes himself as a writer and amateur archaeologist. According to Sergeant McKinley of the Ramsgate police, Foreman is a bit of a crank about everything Chinese. Not only are his house and garden laid out Chinese fashion, but he dresses like a mandarin. And when he goes shopping in Ramsgate he uses a rickshaw drawn by a muscular Chinaman. He paid a lot of money to get the boat from Hong Kong. She has a crew of five: a Scot, a Norwegian, two Irishmen and a Chinese cook."

Inspector van Helder had listened with the utmost attention and he made a few notes. "Someone will have to telephone Sir Keith..."

"I've already done so," exclaimed Tony. "The man himself answered the phone. And he told me right away that he had hired the junk to Galanos for a week, although he'd never rented it to anyone before. And do you know why, sir? Because Galanos persuaded the old man that he's an expert on Chinese art!"

---

fire away!	– dann schieß mal los!
crank	– Kauz, Narr
fashion	– Mode
rickshaw	– Rikscha, Handkarren
to hire	– vermieten
to persuade	– überreden, überzeugen

"In other words, he's bamboozled Sir Keith. Did you find out how much Galanos is paying for the junk?"
"No."
"Well, let's wait and see if shadowing the crew will bring any results. There may be surprises for us all."

The Chinese junk *Su Lin Fu* had been lying at anchor for three days but nothing suspicious had happened so far. The four European members of the crew left the junk every afternoon to enjoy themselves. When they returned, they were usually swaying from side to side and singing. They were never unobserved; every step they took was watched and almost every word they said found its way into the ear of one policeman or another. Yet there was nothing significant in anything they said. They were satisfied with their jobs, because they were well paid for very little work. Sir Keith Foreman may have been an eccentric, but he was obviously not tightfisted. Questioning them openly about Galanos was too risky. If the Greek was really up to mischief, it would be a clear warning to him.
But nothing happened. Every day on the junk was exactly the same as the one before. No visitors called, day or night.
Every morning, at about 9 o'clock, a man who fitted Galanos' description appeared on deck. He would yawn,

---

to bamboozle	– beschwindeln
to shadow	– beschatten
to sway	– schaukeln
unobserved	– unbeobachtet
significant	– bedeutsam
eccentric	– Sonderling
tight-fisted	– knauserig
to be up to mischief	– Böses planen

stretch himself, and pace slowly up and down. Then he would disappear below.
Two hours later, a stocky Chinese figure would come out. The man would take a bicycle and go ashore to do the day's shopping. He always took the same way and visited the same shops in exactly the same order – a bakery, a wholesale spice-merchant's, a butcher's shop, a dairy, a Chinese restaurant and a kiosk selling newspapers and souvenirs. He didn't stay very long at any of these places. And after each of his calls his face beamed as if he had just pulled off the biggest deal in his life.
By now, van Helder knew this routine by heart. What had happened on the twenty-ninth was exactly the same as on the thirtieth and on the thirty-first as well. What or who was Galanos waiting for?
For Jacko Barnelli? If so, where had Barnelli got to? The agent's report made on the morning of the twenty-ninth was still the only information they had about Jacko's presence in Ostend. And Inspector van Helder, growing more and more depressed, kept asking himself if the expense of the operation wasn't too high for an unproved suspicion and a warning from Interpol. After all, including the officers "borrowed" from Ghent and Bruges, he was using more than sixty men on round-the-clock duty in this Barnelli affair.

---

to pace	– schreiten
stocky	– stämmig
wholesale spice-merchant	– Gewürzgroßhändler
dairy	– Milchgeschäft
to beam	– strahlen
to pull off the biggest deal	– das größte Geschäft machen
to grow depressed	– bedrückt werden
he kept asking	– er fragte sich ständig
expense	– (Un)Kosten

Then came the night of the first. It was getting on for 2 a.m.
Jan van Helder, at home in bed, tossed restlessly from side to side. If only he could go asleep...! He had already tried counting sheep and counting backwards from a thousand. He had a feeling that the solution to the case was staring him in the face, and yet it kept eluding him... Barnelli – Galanos – Barnelli – Galanos... He looked at the clock again.
Only 2.10...
Then something clicked. It was like a flash of lightning... He snatched the telephone from beside his bed. Himst answered.
"Is the *Su Lin Fu* still in port?" van Helder roared.
"Why, yes. She's still there, sir. I'd have thought you'd be asleep..."
"So I should be. Any news yet?"
"No, not so far as I know. No trace of Barnelli. Why did you ask about the junk?"
"I've a hunch I'm a little nearer to solving the case. I don't think Galanos will be leaving before mid-day tomorrow... Good night, Tony!"
"Good night, sir," replied Tony Himst, but van Helder had already rung off, leaving his weary colleague rather puzzled.

12.30 p.m.
As usual, Alexis Galanos had appeared on deck at about

---

to toss	– sich hin und her werfen
solution	– Lösung
it kept eluding him	– hier: war nicht zu packen
flash of lightning	– Blitzstrahl
weary	– müde

9 a.m. Maybe he had been a shade nervous and perhaps a shade more hurried.
As usual, the Chinese cook had set off on his bike some two hours later and ridden away towards the bakery. Maybe he, too, had been a shade more nervous, more hurried than usual.
12.30 p.m. Five police officers stepped on board the *Su Lin Fu.* The two Irish sailors who were playing cards stared at them in surprise.
"Chang!" growled a voice from somewhere.
One of the policemen – it was Inspector van Helder – set off in the direction of the voice. His steps led him straight to a luxurious saloon. A man sat over a chart, his back to van Helder. Without turning round, he said: "Tell Murphy we're leaving right away. And where have you been all this time? Any trouble?"
When his question was unanswered, Galanos swung round abruptly. Jan van Helder couldn't help admiring the man's self-control and coolness.
Galanos rose to his feet and made a slight formal bow. He wore an elegant light-grey suit, a white shirt, a silver-grey tie, and a tie-pin with a pink pearl as big as a hazelnut. His speech was as impeccable as his clothing and his manners. "I'm so sorry. I can't have heard you knock, sir!"

---

a shade – ein ganz klein bißchen
to growl – knurren, brummen
chart – See-, Landkarte
to admire – bewundern
slight formal bow – kleine formelle Verbeugung
tie – Schlips
tie-pin – Schlipsnadel
impeccable – untadelig
manners – Benehmen

"I didn't knock. I heard you calling someone and..." Helder left the sentence unfinished.
"I thought that Chang, my cook, had returned."
Van Helder handed Galanos his police identity card.
"Police?" Galanos raised his eyebrows. "What are you looking for on my boat?"
The inspector replaced his card. "If I'm rightly informed, the junk is not yours but the property of Sir Keith Foreman in Ramsgate, England," he said.
Galanos answered: "I've chartered her from Sir Keith. That's not illegal, is it?"
Instead of replying, van Helder looked round the saloon. "Very tastefully furnished, if I may say so. By the way, do you know where your cook is at this moment?"
"He went ashore to do the shopping, and he should have been back long before now. He's very fussy, you know. He insists on buying fresh provisions every day. Unfortunately there's nothing I can do about it. He's one of the crew and I hired him with the junk."
"That's a lie, Mr Galanos!"
Van Helder made his accusation in the mild tone of voice which he might have used to say: "Good morning!" But the effect was anything but cordial.
Alexis Galanos stiffened and his eyes flashed. "How dare you!"
"Of course you're right in saying that the boat's crew

---

identity card – Ausweis
illegal – ungesetzlich
tasteful – geschmackvoll
to furnish – ausstatten, möblieren
to be fussy – wählerisch, heikel sein
provisions – Vorräte
accusation – Anschuldigung
cordial – herzlich

normally includes a Chinese cook, but the regular man was left behind in Ramsgate, as you very well know because you insisted on taking your own cook on this voyage."

Galanos smiled, but did not appear to be in any way overawed. "You seem to be well informed, Inspector."

"Yes, and that's why I'm also in a position to tell you where Chang is now. He's at police headquarters. We've arrested him."

"Arrested him?" Galanos swallowed hard.

"Yes, we took him into custody just as he was once more – buying fresh provisions, as you put it."

"And why has he been arrested?"

Van Helder replied with another question, "Do you know Jacko Barnelli?"

Not a muscle twitched in Galanos' face. "I've never had the pleasure... Am I supposed to know him, Inspector?"

"Not really. It wasn't necessary, not with Chang as your go-between. But you'll soon make the acquaintance of this unknown partner of yours."

"I'm not interested in making Mr Barnelli's acquaintance."

"Alexis Galanos, I'm afraid I must ask you to come with me to headquarters..."

"And what are you charging me with?"

"Receiving stolen goods. We arrested your cook on his daily rounds, together with Jacko Barnelli. Chang had on

---

to overawe	– einschüchtern
to swallow	– schlucken
to twitch	– zucken
go-between	– Mittelsmann
acquaintance	– Bekanntschaft
to charge	– beschuldigen, anklagen

him the last consignment of jewellery, and Barnelli had £ 30,000 in English notes. All we want now is to have back the stolen valuables that have already been handed over to you, and which were brought on board by Chang after his daily shopping expeditions."
Galanos laughed ironically. "And only then will you have any hard evidence against me, Inspector. Otherwise... otherwise you merely *suspect* I may be involved! Would you like me to tell you how many times false suspicion has fallen on me...?"
The inspector nodded. "Yes, that's true... But I promise you that I'll turn the boat inside out. I'll not leave a square centimetre unexamined, I assure you."
Alexis Galanos bowed cynically. "I wish you much joy, Inspector."
The Greek was taken to police headquarters, and immediately ten officers, with some highly experienced customs' officials, began searching the junk from top to bottom. After five hours, not a single piece of the stolen jewellery had come to light. Inspector van Helder grew more and more nervous. If they did not find anything, he would have to release Galanos. Then everything would depend on Chang, on how much he really knew and what he was prepared to say. Not until 10 p.m. did they dis-

---

consignment	– Lieferung
hard evidence	– konkrete Beweise
to involve	– verwickeln
to turn inside out	– das Innere nach außen kehren; gründlichst untersuchen
square centimetre	– Quadratzentimeter
unexamined	– unkontrolliert, ohne Untersuchung
experienced	– erfahren
customs official	– Zollbeamter
to search	– durchsuchen
to release	– frei lassen

cover the hiding-place. It was simple and yet so subtle. The goods were hidden in one of the lifebelts hanging on deck.

Galanos and Chang had exchanged it for one of the boat's genuine lifebelts. The false one contained twelve bags each filled with jewellery and precious stones. Each was marked with an exact, hand-written list of its contents and their value. And each list was in Galanos' own handwriting.

It was getting on for midnight when Galanos confessed. For the Ostend police, this was an enormous scoop. Indeed, it was one of the biggest in their whole history.

As Inspector van Helder was lying sleepless that night, he stumbled on one particular fact that had to do with the shops the Chinese cook visited every day and in the same order. And suddenly the inspector had a hunch that Chang must be meeting Jacko Barnelli in one of these places. As we now know, this suspicion was correct.

Which do you think was the place where Inspector van Helder arrested the Chinese cook Chang and the jewel-thief Barnelli? If you think it over carefully there can be only one *correct answer.*

---

subtle – fein, schlau
lifebelt – Rettungsring
to exchange – austauschen
to contain – enthalten
contents – Inhalt
value – Wert
to confess – gestehen
scoop – Fang

5 The man who looked like a bulldog

For three days mist and fog had shrouded the German–Austrian border. In the Salzburg area not a single mountain peak could be seen from the valley. It was the kind of weather when everybody tried to avoid going out of doors.
The clock stood at eleven minutes past six that evening when a stranger entered the empty bar of the village inn, *The Old Customs House*. He was of medium build and wore a dark green coat, small boots and an old leather hat, which he immediately took off and tossed on to the hat-rack.
As he wiped his forehead with a huge handkerchief, he saw Xaver Bernhuber coming out of the kitchen.
It was clearly something of an effort for the visitor to force a smile on his flat, ugly face with its squashed nose and deep folds.
"Are you the landlord?" he asked curtly.
Bernhuber, the innkeeper, gazed down on him with a

---

fog	– (Nebel-)Dunst
to shroud	– einhüllen, verschleiern
border	– Grenze
peak	– Gipfel
to avoid	– vermeiden
of medium build	– von mittlerer Größe
hat-rack	– Hutablage
effort	– Anstrengung
squashed	– platt gedrückt
fold	– Falte
landlord	– Gastwirt

mixture of curiosity and politeness. “That’s right,” he nodded.
“Would you by any chance have a room for a traveller accidentally stranded here?”
Bernhuber nodded again. “The answer’s ‘yes’, if you don’t expect too much, that is. I can only offer you a simple room, I’m afraid. No running hot water or telephones here, you know. How long will you be staying?”
The stranger shrugged.
“If the weather stays like this, I’ll be off tomorrow, I expect...” He threw up his hands impatiently. “But my car has broken down,” he grumbled. “I had to leave it by the side of the road, a couple of kilometres from here... And it was just serviced, too!”
“Dear dear,” sighed Bernhuber politely. “Mechanics these days... But how did you get here, then?”
“Shanks’s pony, of course... And I hate nothing more than walking. Is there a garage nearby that does repairs?”
“No. The nearest one is in Piding,” replied the landlord, who suddenly realized what the stranger reminded him of: a bulldog! Yes, that squashed face, with the deep folds... Even his way of speaking fitted the picture: a harsh, hoarse voice like a dog barking.
“Could you look up the number for me?” asked the

---

by any chance	– vielleicht, zufällig
accidentally	– zufällig(erweise)
running hot water	– fließend warmes Wasser
to shrug	– mit der Schulter zucken
to grumble	– murren, schimpfen
it was serviced	– es war in der Werkstatt
to sigh	– seufzen
shank’s pony	– auf Schusters Rappen, zu Fuß
harsh	– rauh
hoarse	– heiser

"bulldog", and Xaver Bernhuber reached for the telephone directory.

Soon the guest was barking into the mouthpiece: "My name is Born, Alfons Born, and I'm staying at *The Old Customs House*. My car has broken down and I've had to leave it about two kilometres down the road from here. Could you send someone to find out what's wrong with it?"

The man at the other end of the line explained that everyone else in the garage had already gone home, and that he himself would have to see to it. But that he wouldn't be able to get away for at least another hour. The bulldog who answered to the name of Born agreed to wait and rang off.

"Would you like something to eat, Mr Born?" asked the landlord.

Yes, Mr Born would, and in the course of the following hour he completely destroyed the landlord's illusion that small men have small appetites. Born set to work with a will. As well as three toasted sandwiches and two pretzels, he demolished four large pieces of bread, a cold pork chop, and a huge plate of sliced sausage, on which he sprinkled so much pepper that just to see it brought tears to the landlord's eyes. This huge meal was washed down with three tankards of beer. Xaver Bernhuber could't get over it. He would never have believed there was room for so much food inside the little "bulldog".

---

telephone directory	– Telefonbuch
to destroy	– zerstören
with a will	– mit Lust und Liebe
to demolish	– vernichten; hier: verschlingen
pork chop	– Schweinekotelette
plate of sliced sausage	– Wurstplatte
tankard	– Krug

Slowly the bar filled with customers, and at about half-past seven the man from the garage in Piding appeared to collect Born's car-keys. Half an hour later he was back again, and the expression on his face was a mixture of scorn and anger as he stood beside Born's table.
"Are you trying to pull my leg or something?" he asked.
The "bulldog" looked astonished. "Why should I do that?"
"Because of the car."
"What about the car?"
"You said there was something wrong, that you'd broken down..."
"That's right. It stopped – just wouldn't go."
The man from the garage grinned contemptuously and the "bulldog" grew annoyed. "What was the matter then?"
"You'd run out of petrol."
Born's jaw dropped, and an incredulous look came into his eyes.
"No petrol?" he asked.
"That's what I said. Here are your keys, and here's my bill."
"Where's my car now?"
"Exactly where you left it. I put in ten litres for you. That should be enough to get you to the nearest filling-station.

---

to collect	– abholen
scorn	– Verachtung
to pull one's leg	– jemanden zum Narren halten
contemptuous(ly)	– verächtlich
grew annoyed	– wurde ärgerlich
you'd run out of petrol	– Ihnen ist das Benzin ausgegangen
jaw	– Kiefer
incredulous	– ungläubig
bill	– Rechnung

But if you expect me to bring the car here, it'll cost you another twenty Marks."
Mr Born agreed at once. He paid the bill and the additional twenty Marks, and even added a tip of ten Marks. Fifteen minutes later, his car stood in the courtyard of *The Old Customs House.*
He then ate four large saveloys, together with a whole glass of horseradish, drank another two tankards of beer, stuck a couple of newspapers under one arm and climbed the stairs to his room on the top floor.
The new day dawned as the old one had ended: grey and misty.
A few minutes past seven, the yellow mail-van arrived with a telegram for Mr Alfons Born. As the bulldog did not want to be called until eight o'clock, the landlord placed the telegram in the letter-rack. At half-past seven, the usual postman arrived, bringing the mail and the daily papers.
Fifteen minutes later, the four Axenmeyer brothers appeared at the bar. They knocked on the counter, demanding their usual breakfast. They did this regularly every morning while they were working as lumberjacks in the wood near by. As Bernhuber was serving the men, he grew more and more silent and thoughtful. An idea had occurred to him, and he was so preoccupied with it that

---

additional	– zusätzlich
tip	– Trinkgeld
saveloy	– Zervelatwurst(brot)
horseradish	– Meerrettich
letter-rack	– Brieffach
lumberjack	– Holzfäller
to occur	– (über)kommen
preoccupied	– beschäftigt, gefangen

he forgot to call Mr Born at the pre-arranged time.
At 8.15 a.m., the brothers left, and Xaver picked up the telephone. Inspector Lambert, whom he had known for some time, answered it. "Yes, Mr Bernhuber? What's wrong?"
Bernhuber looked carefully round before he said: "I have to whisper. Can you hear me like this?"
"Yes, I can hear you all right," the inspector said.
"Last night a man arrived here and took a room. His name is Alfons Born and, as he told me his car had broken down. Later on it turned out that he'd simply run out of petrol... But there's something fishy about his story, Inspector."
"Where is he now?"
"He's still asleep upstairs. But I can describe him to you easily."
"How do you mean?"
Xaver Bernhuber couldn't help laughing. "He looks exactly like a bulldog!"
The inspector's cool politeness was abruptly replaced by keen interest. His questions became very pointed. "Is your Mr Born short and plump?"
"Yes, I'm two heads taller than he is."
"Has he cropped grey hair, very short?"
"Yes."
"And is his voice rather hoarse? I mean, does it sound a bit like a dog barking?"

---

pre-arranged – vorher abgesprochen
to turn out – sich herausstellen
fishy – komisch, verdächtig, faul
to replace – ersetzen, weichen
pointed – gezielt
cropped hair – kurzgeschnittenes Haar

The landlord was so surprised that he nodded with excitement instead of answering, so the inspector couldn't hear. "I say, Mr Bernhuber!" he shouted. "Are you still there?"

"Yes, and you're right; it does sound like barking when he speaks. But how do you know all this? Is he someone you know?"

"I'll say! And his name isn't Born either – it's Dixler. Make sure he doesn't get away, that's all. We'll come over right away."

It didn't take long before three police officers arrived at *The Old Customs House.* While two of them hustled the furious Dixler, alias Born, into the police car, Inspector Lambert explained things to the surprised landlord. "That was very clever of you to inform us, Mr Bernhuber. Thousands of people in your position wouldn't have smelt a rat. Do you know, we've been after Dixler for more than three months."

"What's he been up to?"

"Passing forged notes."

"Forged notes!" echoed Bernhuber, and in his mind's eye he could still see the bulldog before him stuffing down mountains of toasted sandwiches and sausage.

"And on a very large scale, too," the inspector went on. "And now I'm convinced that before the morning's over we'll have the rest of the gang in the bag."

---

to hustle	– stoßen, drängen
to smell the rat	– den Braten riechen
forged	– gefälscht
to pass	– in Umlauf bringen
trap	– Falle
soil	– Boden
to arouse	– erwecken

And this turned out to be true. Three men, with a large consignment of forged banknotes, ran straight into the trap set for them as soon as they stepped on Germain soil.

And now, Super Sleuths, what was the mistake made by the bulldog that aroused the landlord's suspicions?

6 The smugglers

It was quite difficult to get a copy of the written examination paper, set by the Argus College of Crime Detection at Little Covenbridge. The college trains young people who would like to become super sleuths. The title of this paper is The Smugglers, and here it is:

Luigi Amati and Enrico Sardo had worked out for themselves an original way of smuggling valuables between two neighbouring countries. At noon, when the sun is at its zenith and casts the longest shadows, they would push out their boat into the water of a lake and let themselves drift with the current towards the middle. This lake is the frontier between the two countries, and it is said to be one of the few inland waters fed entirely by subterranean springs.
Once Amati and Sardo had reached the half-way point, they used to start fishing. And they would go on doing so until darkness fell. Now and again they would even catch a few sea-trout, which they gutted at once and packed away in cold-bags.

---

examination paper	– Prüfungsarbeit
to set	– stellen, aufgeben
College of Crime Detection	– Fachschule für Verbrechensaufklärung
valuables	– Wertsachen
to cast	– werfen
current	– Strömung
subterranean spring	– unterirdische Quelle
sea-trout	– Meer-, Lachsforelle
to gut	– ausnehmen
cold bag	– Kühlbeutel

Just as evening was turning into night, the two men would spring into action. With swift strokes of the oars they would make for the opposite shore, where a contact man would be already waiting for them.
Together they would beach the boat, turn it upside down and fasten a watertight canister to the bottom. Its contents were invariably two hundred watches.
This Friday in September was no exception. Everything went without a hitch – as it had always done before.
At ten past midnight they began to row back across the lake. They landed at a point half a kilometre north of the place where they usually kept their boat and they opened the canister. Then they divided the smuggled goods fairly, that is, ten dozen watches for each of them.

to beach – ans Ufer ziehen
invariably – konstant, unveränderlich
without a hitch – reibungslos

Five minutes later they had vanished into the darkness. All they had left behind were two pairs of boots and a faint smell of fish. And when a customs patrol found the boat around midnight, there was nothing to cause any suspicion.

And yet it turned out to be Black Friday for the two smugglers after all. They had no idea at the time that, by coincidence, just as they were making their getaway a burglar had broken into a jeweller's shop in the centre of the town and made a clean sweep. The police had arranged a widespread search over the whole area. And our friends Luigi and Enrico ran straight into one of the patrols at the very moment when they were only too anxious to avoid the police.

It may be added that the crime squad were as delighted with their success as the smugglers were disgusted with their bad luck.

How many factual mistakes are contained in this test paper from the Argus College of Crime Detection, Little Covenbridge?

---

to cause	– verursachen
by coincidence	– durch Zufall
to make one's getaway	– abhauen
to make a clean sweep	– reinen Tisch machen
crime squad	– Verbrechensabteilung
disgusted	– verärgert
factual mistakes	– sachliche Fehler

7 A car accident

It was just before 8 p.m. when they collided. The cyclist was to blame, there was no doubt about it. He now stood disconsolately beside his wrecked bicycle, swearing under his breath.

The car driver, for his part, was looking at the car's shattered blinker and the scratches on its wing. The cyclist grumbled: "You needn't act as if it were all my fault. It was just as much yours."

Robert Kessing, the driver of the car, looked at the cyclist calmly. "I should let the police decide whose fault it was," he replied, without raising his voice. "One thing is certain: you shot out of that entrance like a madman without looking left or right."

The cyclist denied it hotly. "You'll have to prove that. There weren't any witnesses." He gazed furtively up and down the street, but it was not a main road and there was little traffic. The few inquisitive people who had paused earlier had all gone away by now. "Well, where *are* your witnesses?" he asked defiantly, with a swift glance at the block of flats opposite.

---

to collide	– zusammenstoßen
disconsolate(ly)	– untröstlich
to swear	– fluchen
to shatter	– zerschmettern
scratch	– Kratzer
wing	– Kotflügel
to deny	– leugnen
furtive(ly)	– verstohlen, heimlich
defiant(ly)	– herausfordernd
swift glance	– rascher Blick
block of flats	– Wohnblock

At that moment the police patrol car came round the corner.
"You've taken your time, I must say!" were Mr Kessing's first words to the two officers.
"Sorry, sir," replied Sergeant Horn. "There was a hold-up in the tunnel under the river and we couldn't get through."
The officers took statements, measured the skidmarks and estimated the damage, which was not very serious. The cyclist seemed relieved when he was allowed to go. He snatched up his wreck of a bike, shouldered it and made off.
Sergeant Horn turned to the driver. "You see, Mr..." – here he glanced quickly at his notebook – "Mr Kessing, it's your word against his. But you mentioned something about a witness a moment ago."
"Yes, there was a woman who saw what happened, sergeant. As I got out of the car, I saw her looking out of a window across the road. From that big block of flats – on the second floor, the end window on the left."
The sergeant nodded. "Let's try our luck."
The name on the door was Marquand. It was only after they had rung three times that the door was opened. An elderly grey-haired woman stood before them. She looked at Kessing with hostility, and allowed the men to enter only after protesting vigorously. "Well? What do

---

you've taken...	– Sie haben lange gebraucht
hold-up	– Stau
skidmark	– Bremsspur
to estimate	– schätzen
relieved	– erleichtert
hostility	– Feindseligkeit
vigorous(ly)	– heftig

you want?" she asked defiantly.
"It's about the accident," explained the officer.
"What accident?"
Mr Kessing was at a loss. "But you saw what happened from your window. You even shook your head," he stammered.
"You must be mistaken. You've mixed me up with someone else."
Mr Kessing hesitated. "But I recognize you perfectly," he insisted after a moment.
At this point Sergeant Horn intervened. "Are you saying you've never seen this gentleman before?"
"Never!"
"Nor the other man involved?"
"No. I didn't know the cyclist either."
The policeman in his turn seemed as much at a loss as Kessing had been.
"Now look here, Mrs Marquand," he said sharply. "Why should this gentleman say that he saw you at the window if it isn't true?"
The woman turned away grumbling. "You'd better ask him, not me. In any case, I've been far too busy today to stand there staring out of the window."
"She's telling lies," declared Mr Kessing angrily.
For a moment it looked as if the woman would throw something at Robert Kessing. Then she thought better of it. Scornfully she replied: "We'll soon see who's telling lies!"
At this, Sergeant Horn drew himself up to his full height.

---

to be at a loss	– in Verlegenheit sein
to hesitate	– zögern
to insist	– beharren, bestehen auf
drew himself up to…	– richtete er sich zur vollen Größe auf

"We know that already, madam," he corrected her. "You're the one who's lying."
"But..."

At this point the story ends for Super Sleuths to find out how Sergeant Horn knew Mrs Marquand wasn't speaking the truth.

8 A talking doll

Chief Inspector Joost van Druisen of the Amsterdam Drug Squad was at his wit's end. For the sixth time that year – it was now August – he had got information from his most trusted agent that an exceptionally large consignment of illegal drugs must have arrived at the port of Rotterdam. As was usual in such cases, he at once ordered a major search operation. But in spite of the most thorough and widespread enquiries, this latest raid, too, was not very successful. Only a total of twenty-nine kilogrammes of hashish had been discovered and confiscated. But where was all the rest? From which country had it come? From which city? On which ships? How did the whole criminal organization work? Questions... Questions and even more questions that van Druisen still could not answer.

Eventually – and by this time it was 21 October – a small ray of hope gleamed on the horizon: the police succeeded in arresting one of the main culprits. He was Jan Kenatzki who was ready to "sing".

From him van Druisen discovered two facts. The first was that the mastermind who held all the threads in his hands actually lived in Amsterdam. Kenatzki however knew neither the name nor the address of his mysterious chief,

---

at one's wits end	– am Ende seiner Weisheit
exceptional(ly)	– außergewöhnlich
drug	– Droge
thorough enquiry	– gründliche Untersuchung
raid	– Razzia
ray of hope	– Hoffnungsschimmer
mastermind	– Kopf, Chef

because all the "When," "Where" and "How much"-instructions were given by telephone. In other words, he knew the key figure only by his voice. But the second piece of information was much the more important. Kenatzki had only stumbled on it by accident. This was that a Frenchman called Mertier arrived at Amsterdam airport on the fifth of every month. He appeared to be the courier from head office, who brought in coded form all the details about the consignments – exact quantities, dates, routing, and so on – to the boss in Amsterdam.
Joost van Druisen was too much of a sceptic to rejoice prematurely. But nevertheless he felt a bit excited at the thought of the fifth of the following month. Only two weeks to go, and then, perhaps...

5 November. All preparations were complete. The security network was so tight that only a man on a flying carpet could have slipped through.
The plane from Paris was due to land at 10.25 a.m. Air France had already confirmed that a certain Henry Mertier was aboard the Boeing 727.
The Chief inspector's plan was as follows: as Mertier's identity was not known, it had been arranged with the officers checking passports to indicate which passenger was Mertier. Thereafter, it was hoped that Mertier would lead the police straight to the mysterious chief.
10.40 a.m. One of the officers raised his cap. That was the agreed signal! So the rather stocky man with a Medi-

---

head office	– Zentrale
to rejoice prematurely	– zu früh frohlocken
tight	– eng, dicht
was due to...	– sollte...
to confirm	– bestätigen
to indicate	– ein Zeichen geben

terranean appearance must be Henry Mertier.
He was carrying a small case and leading a little girl by the hand. She was about five years old, with shoulder-length black hair. She never stopped chattering for a moment, and she was hugging a big talking doll.
Mertier hailed a taxi.

The large elegant house with an extensive garden was surrounded by more than thirty police officers. Exactly a minute earlier, a man had appeared at the front door and admitted Mertier into the house, together with the child.
Chief Inspector van Druisen rang the bell. This time a young woman opened the door. She seemed to be a housemaid, for she held a duster in her left hand.
Van Druisen pushed aside the surprised girl, showed her his police card and whispered: "Crime Investigation Squad. Please keep your voice down. Where is Monsieur Mertier?"
The maid began trembling and pointed to a door. "He's with D ... D ... Doc ..." she whispered, stammering nervously.
"With Dr van Geldern?" asked van Druisen.
This time the maid only nodded.
Together with three of his men, the chief inspector went to his door, knocked once and opened it without waiting.

Mediterranean appearance	– südländisches Aussehen
to chatter	– reden, quasseln
to hug	– im Arm halten
to hail	– heranwinken
extensive	– weitläufig
to admit	– hier: hereinlassen
crime investigation squad	– Abteilung zur Verbrechensbekämpfung

TAXI

Mertier and the little girl, Nanette, had not yet taken off their coats and the child was still holding her doll. Dr van Geldern and his guest each had a glass of whisky in one hand, and they appeared to be drinking one another's health.

The police officer introduced himself.

"Crime Investigation Squad? What does this mean?" asked van Geldern, frowning.

"I have here a warrant for the arrest of Monsieur Henry Mertier."

Neither Mertier nor the doctor seemed particularly upset. Van Geldern turned coolly to his desk, and as he lifted the telephone receiver he said: "I'm ringing my friend, the French consul. I'm sure he'll be interested."

The chief inspector nodded. "Of course you may phone the French consul. And you can tell him he is allowed to visit Monsieur Mertier at any time at police headquarters..." And with a charming smile van Druisen continued quickly: "And if your friend the consul isn't in too much of a hurry, he may also pay you a visit at the same place. I hope you appreciate my cooperative attitude."

Dr van Geldern replaced the receiver. His face looked suddenly ashen. "What exactly do you mean?"

"Within the hour I'll have a warrant for your arrest too – as well as a search warrant for the house which at the moment is of even greater interest to me."

"What crime am I supposed to have committed?"

---

health	– Gesundheit, Wohl
warrant	– Vollmacht
particularly upset	– besonders bestürzt
appreciate	– schätzen
cooperative attitude	– Entgegenkommen
ashen	– aschfahl
...am I supposed to...	– soll ich begangen haben

"Trafficking in drugs, Dr van Geldern."
The other man laughed harshly. "I think you're going to regret this, Chief Inspector!"
And it almost looked that way. For the Chief Inspector's search was a complete failure and he looked like making a complete fool of himself. It was 8.45 p.m. by now – and he had found absolutely nothing.
"Are you really certain you haven't overlooked anything?" the chief inspector asked one of his most reliable specialists.
The specialist nodded. "I'm certain. We've tested everything. The X-ray photographs were completely negative. If my team can't find anything, then there are definitely no drugs in the house."
"What about the child?"
"Mrs Hellgersen has searched her, too."
Mrs Hellgersen was called in. As if she had been waiting for her cue, she said quickly: "A charming little thing – and so friendly. But I found nothing on her."
"What about the doll?" thundered van Druisen, nearly at the end of his tether.
"It's a perfectly ordinary talking doll. We've tested its clothes, we've twisted off its head, and taken it to pieces – but without any result. All that happened is that the child yelled her head off. Of course one of the boys went out and bought her a new one – the same kind naturally."

---

trafficking	– Handel
to regret	– bedauern
failure	– Mißerfolg
x-ray	– Röntgenstrahl
cue	– Stichwort
at the end of his tether	– am Ende seiner Kraft
to yell one's head off	– wie am Spieß brüllen

Then she added quietly: "I've left the receipt for it on your desk, sir." For three minutes the chief inspector paced the room. Suddenly he stopped. An unlikely idea had struck him.
With three steps he was standing in front of the woman police officer. "Where's that doll now?"
"It's still in my cupboard!" replied Anita Hellgersen stepping back in alarm.
"Fetch it!"
Five minutes later, van Druisen was giving three cheers. He had found the answer. A strikingly simple solution. Everything he wanted to know was literally lying before him...
And months later the police were still discussing why they hadn't thought of it before...

Where did Chief Inspector van Druisen find the solution to the case?

---

receipt	– Quittung
unlikely	– unwahrscheinlich
to give three cheers	– hurra schreien
strikingly	– bestechend
literally	– im wahrsten Sinn des Wortes

9 A ransom demand

London, 19 September, 9.20 a.m.
John Mitchell, fifty-three years old, frowned angrily as the telephone rang. "Yes, Kathie, who is it?" he asked, a shade more sharply than he had intended.
"Your wife wants to speak to you, sir. I'll put her through."
Mitchell's face cheered up at once. "Hello, Diana darling, I didn't expect you to call so early."
No reply.
Mitchell hesitated, beginning to feel uneasy. "Diana? Hello there. What's wrong?"
His wife's voice was interrupted by tears. "John... John... it's terrible... something awful has happened... it's..."
Mitchell felt his throat tighten. He could hardly breathe. Then another voice could be heard on the line – a man's voice, muffled and disguised. "Listen carefully, Mr Mitchell. If you don't want your wife to come to any harm, do exactly as I tell you."
"But what..." exclaimed Mitchell.
"Don't interrupt!" barked the voice. "You'll go straight to your bank in Richmond Street when this call is over. There you will draw out £ 20,000 in small notes. Then re-

---

ransom demand – Lösegeldforderung
to put through – (telefonisch) weiter verbinden
to tighten – zusammenziehen
muffled – gedämpft
disguised – verstellt
to come to harm – zu Schaden kommen
to draw out – (Geld) abheben

turn to your office. The time is now 9.23 precisely. You'll be back at your desk by ten o'clock. At 10.15, a Mr Arthur Wilcox will call. Hand the money over to him..."
John Mitchell's voice grew husky. "I want to speak to my wife... please..."
Silence. Then: "John, John... help me, I beg you... please, help me... help me..." Diana's voice stopped abruptly as the receiver was replaced.
With trembling hands, Mitchell dialled his home number. Engaged.
A moment later he tried again, but he needed several attempts, for his trembling fingers kept misdialling. Once more the number was engaged. Obviously the receiver had been taken off.
Mitchell looked at his watch. 9.24. It flashed through his mind that the ought to ring the police... Should he? No, he rejected the idea as quickly as it had come.
He got up. His legs felt heavy and stiff, while the lump in his throat seemed to get thicker and thicker. When he went into the outer office, Kathie Hamilton stared at the pale face of her boss as if he were a ghost. He made an effort to smile. "I'm just going to the bank," he muttered. It was only after he had left that she answered his statement with a nod.
John Mitchell, owner of a famous London goldsmith's, crossed St Patrick's Street as if in a trance. He went into one of the shops there, Bolton and Redford's, and bought a small blue case. Then he turned in the direction of

---

husky – heiser
engaged – besetzt
to dial – wählen
to misdial – falsch wählen
to reject – verwerfen
lump – Kloß, 'Frosch'

Richmond Street. At every step he could hear his wife's voice: "John... John, I beg you... help me... help me..." He walked faster, but the voice dogged him still: "John... please... help me... help me..."
At 9.55 he was back in his office, sitting at the mahogany desk, shivering. 9.56... 9.57...
Every ten seconds he looked at his watch automatically. 9.59...
Hesitantly he groped for the telephone, took the receiver with a cautious movement and dialled – dialled his own number. But it was no use...
10.10. Only five more minutes to go. His eyes were fixed to the case lying on the visitor's chair. £ 20,000. A lot of money. Yet when he thought of his wife, Diana, it seemed a small price.
10.15. Where was that man Wilcox? It was only then that Mitchell realized his forehead was damp with sweat.
The telephone.
Mitchell snatched up the receiver and heard Kathie's calm, even voice say: "A Mr Arthur Wilcox to see you, Sir. Shall I send him in?"
"Yes, send him in."
The man who entered looked like a perfect English gentleman, both in his elegantly tailored suit and also in his bearing. Mitchell thought him to be about thirty years old.
The stranger nodded curtly. "My name is Wilcox!" he announced, looking Mitchell straight in the eye with an icy stare. "The money, if you please."

---

to dog	– verfolgen
to shiver	– zittern, frösteln
to grope for	– tasten nach
damp	– feucht

Mitchel tried to get to his feet, but his legs refused to obey him.
"And my wife?" he asked.
"She's alive, and if you're sensible she'll remain so after this little matter is all over." A scornful smile played round the blackmailer's lips.
"What do you mean, sensible?" said Mitchell with a trembling voice.
"Listen. On the opposite side of the street is a telephone booth – you can see it from your window. From there I shall ring my partner. After I've left the booth, wait another five minutes... After that, you can phone your wife... or even the police for all I care. But if you ring one minute sooner" – Wilcox stepped forward a pace, and his eyes had a wild gleam in them – "one minute sooner, and you won't see your wife alife again!"
Mitchell was frozen with horror.
"For the last time, Mr Mitchell, the money."
The terrified man pointed to the case. Wilcox opened it, looked at the contents, and gave a satisfied nod. "Nice meeting you!" And the blackmailer had gone.
John Mitchell waited a moment before darting to the window, then back to his desk to call his home, which was still engaged, and returning to the window once more. Wilcox was crossing the road. He entered the telephone box, lifted the receiver, dialled, put a coin in the slot and then hung up again.
As he left the box, he waved to Mitchell who hastily drew back from the window. He looked at his watch: another

---

sensible	– vernünftig
blackmailer	– Erpresser
for all I care	– meinetwegen
to dart	– rennen, stürzen

Telephone

five minutes... When he dialled yet again, there was still the engaged tone.

Exactly six minutes later Mitchell called the police. Then he ran down to get his car.

A traffic-jam in Rackland Road held him up for almost twenty minutes. John Melville Mitchell felt he'd go mad...

Mitchell's wife, Diana, was pale and trembling. With her was Inspector Garnett of Scotland Yard. Garnett had been waiting impatiently.

"So sorry", muttered Mitchell breathlessly, "a traffic-jam in Rackland Road, no one could move..."

Garnett nodded. "Your wife has told me the whole story. We've no time to lose..."

"I kept trying to phone but the line was engaged," explained Mitchell.

Diana sobbed. "The man who rang you did something to the phone. I wanted to call you when he'd gone, but it wouldn't work."

The inspector interrupted. "You can discuss all that later. What I need now, Mr Mitchell, is that you describe the exact appearance of this man who came to see you, and also that of the case you gave him containing the money. Please be precise. Every detail is vital."

Mitchell looked helplessly at his wife, who was now crying softly. But she nodded to him bravely. "I'm better, darling, really I am... Now you must help the inspector all you can."

And so Mitchell gave his account of his terrible experience, from the beginning until his arrival home.

---

traffic-jam – Stau
account – Bericht

Twelve hours later. It was getting on for midnight...
Diana was pouring out a whisky for her husband, who suddenly grew silent. He rose abruptly, went over to the telephone, and rang Scotland Yard. When he had rung off, his wife looked at him with dark, frightened eyes.
"But John!" she exclaimed. "Why should you ask Inspector Garnett to come out here again at this time of night?"
Mitchell's look was firm but sad as he replied: "To interrogate you, Diana."
The heavy whisky glass fell to the floor.
"Me?"
"Yes, Diana. I've just realized that you are hand in glove with that fellow Wilcox. And that no one else was ever involved..."

A very difficult case. If you can solve it you really are a Super Sleuth. The question to be answered is: what made Mitchell realize his wife was involved?

---

to interrogate – verhören
to be hand in glove – unter einer Decke stecken
to solve – lösen

Solutions

The case of the stolen paintings, page 7.
It must have taken place in Britain, where the distances are measured in miles, and the traffic drives on the left.

Bring on the clowns!, page 10.
Detective-Sergeant Watzmann decided that Hempell was most likely to be the culprit. This was because he knew two facts that had not so far been mentioned. These were that the case had to do with money taken from the ring-master's caravan, and also that the thief was known to have been dressed as a clown.

The squatters who got a fright, page 15.
Our friend Sid made a big mistake when he lit a huge log fire: the clearly visible smoke from the chimney gave the game away.

The secret of the Chinese junk, page 19.
Inspector van Helder's hunch was that the meetings took place at the wholesale spice-merchant's. And he turned out to be right, for that was where Chang and Barnelli were caught red-handed.
Nobody will buy "fresh" spices day after day. They last a long time and in any case every kitchen keeps a stock of spices on hand. Besides, why would he bother to buy spices wholesale for such a small number of people?

The man who looked like a bulldog, page 33.
Born (or rather Dixler!) told the innkeeper that he was accidentally stranded in that area. That this was a lie became apparent to the landlord when the telegram arrived next morning. The "bulldog's" only telephone call on the evening before had been to the garage. So how could the sender of the telegram have known where Dixler would be spending the night unless it had been prearranged?

The smugglers, page 42.
The test paper contains five factual errors:
1 When the sun is at its zenith it casts no shadows, neither short ones nor long ones.
2 A lake fed entirely by subterranean springs would not have a current.
3 Sea-trout are salt-water fish.
4 The number of watches smuggled was two hundred, not two hundred and forty, so the two men couldn't have shared the total equally and still have ten dozen each.
5 It was ten past midnight when the smugglers started rowing back, so a customs patrol couldn't have found their boat on the opposite shore at midnight.

A car accident, page 45.
If Mrs Marquand hadn't witnessed the accident she couldn't have known that the other man involved was a cyclist.

A talking doll, page 50.
On the tape inside the talking doll had been recorded all the information the police wanted.

A ransom demand, page 57.

After the first telephone conversation with his wife, John Mitchell had not been able to speak with her again until he returned home. And in his call to the police he had given no details. But when he reached his house, the inspector at once asked him to describe the man and "the case containing the money". This could mean only one thing – that the officer had heard of the case from Diana, who in turn could only have heard of it from Wilcox himself.

---

most likely – höchstwahrscheinlich
gave the game away – verriet sich
to catch s. o. red-handed – jemand auf frischer Tat ertappen
stock – Vorrat
apparent – offenbar, klar
unless – es sei denn
tape – Tonband

Vocabulary

A	absentminded ['æbsənt'maindid]	– geistesabwesend
	to accelerate [æg'sæləreit]	– beschleunigen
	accidental(ly) [æksi'dentl]	– zufällig(erweise)
	accomplice [ə'kɔmplis]	– Komplice
	account [ə'kaunt]	– Bericht
	accusation [ækju:'zeiʃn]	– Anschuldigung
	acquaintance [ə'kweintəns]	– Bekanntschaft
	to acquire [ə'kwaiə]	– gewinnen
	additional [ə'diʃnl]	– zusätzlich
	to admire [əd'maiə]	– bewundern
	to admit [əd'mit]	– hier: hereinlassen
	to alter ['ɔ:ltə]	– ändern
	to annoy [ə'nɔi]	– ärgern
	apparent [ə'pærənt]	– offenbar, klar
	appearance [ə'piərəns]	– Erscheinung
	to appreciate [ə'pri:ʃieit]	– schätzen
	archaeologist [ɑ:ki'ɔlədʒist]	– Archäologe
	to arouse [ə'rauz]	– erwecken
	ashen [æʃn]	– aschfahl
	authentic [ɔ:'θentik]	– echt
	to avoid [ə'vɔid]	– vermeiden
B	to bamboozle [bæm'bu:zl]	– beschwindeln, übers Ohr hauen
	to beam [bi:m]	– strahlen
	bill [bil]	– Rechnung
	blackmailer ['blækmeilə]	– Erpresser
	to blaze [bleiz]	– glühen, brennen
	border ['bɔ:də]	– Grenze
	bow [bau]	– Verbeugung
C	calm [ka:m]	– ruhig
	cash [kæʃ]	– Klein-, Wechselgeld
	to cast [ka:st]	– werfen

to cause [kɔːz]	– verursachen
caution [kɔːʃn]	– Vorsicht
by any chance [tʃaːns]	– vielleicht, zufällig
to charge [tʃaːdʒ]	– beschuldigen, anklagen
chart [tʃaːt]	– (Land-, See-)Karte
to chatter ['tʃætə]	– reden, quasseln
to circulate ['səːkjuleit]	– i. Umlauf sein
bei coincidence [kou'insidəns]	– zufällig
to collect [kə'lekt]	– einsammeln, abholen
to collide [kə'laid]	– zusammenstoßen
compound ['kɔmpaund]	– Gelände, Platz, Gehege
conclusion [kɔn'kluːʒn]	– Schlußfolgerung
to confess [kɔn'fes]	– gestehen
to confirm [kən'fəːm]	– bestätigen
consignment [kən'sainmənt]	– Lieferung
to contain [kɔn'tein]	– enthalten
contemptuous [kən'temptjuəs]	– verächtlich
contents ['kɔntents]	– Inhalt
cordial ['kɔːdjəl]	– herzlich
cosy ['kouzi]	– gemütlich
cowl [kaul]	– Kutte
to crack [kræk]	– knacken, hier: als falsch beweisen
to crackle [krækl]	– knistern
craftsman ['kraːftsmən]	– Handwerker
crammed [kræmd]	– vollgestopft
crank [krænk]	– Kauz, Narr
crime [kraim]	– Verbrechen
crisp [krisp]	– forsch
cropped [krɔpt]	– kurzgeschnitten
cruise [kruːz]	– (See-)Reise, Vergnügungsfahrt
cue [kjuː]	– Stichwort
culprit ['kʌlprit]	– Schuldige(r)
current ['kʌrənt]	– Strömung

	custody ['kʌstədi]	– Bewachung
	customs ['kʌstəmz]	– Zoll
D	dagger ['dægə]	– Dolch
	to look ~s at	– mit Blicken durchbohren
	dainty ['deinti]	– zierlich
	dairy ['dεəri]	– Milchgeschäft
	damp [dæmp]	– feucht
	daring ['dεəriŋ]	– wagemutig
	to dart [daːt]	– rennen, stürzen
	deal [diːl]	– Geschäft, Handel
	debts [dets]	– Schulden
	defiant [di'faiənt]	– herausfordernd
	to demand [dimaːnd]	– in Anspruch nehmen, fordern
	to demolish [di'mɔliʃ]	– vernichten, hier: verschlingen
	to deny [di'nai]	– leugnen
	depressed [di'prest]	– bedrückt, niedergeschlagen
	to destroy [di'strɔi]	– zerstören
	to devour [di'vauə]	– verschlingen
	to dial ['daiəl]	– wählen (Tel.)
	directory [dai'rektəri]	– Telefonbuch
	disconsolate(ly) [dis'kɔnsəlit]	– untröstlich
	to disguise [dis'gaiz]	– verstellen, verkleiden
	disgusted [dis'gʌstid]	– verärgert
	to dismiss [dis'mis]	– entlassen, hier: vom Tisch fegen
	to disturb [dis'təːb]	– stören
	to dog [dɔg]	– verfolgen
	to doubt [daut]	– bezweifeln
	to draw [drɔː]	– hier: (Geld) abheben
	drug [drʌg]	– Droge, Rauschgift
	due [djuː]	– fällig, erwartet
E	eccentric [ik'sentrik]	– Sonderling
	effort ['efət]	– Anstrengung

	to elude [i'lu:d]	– entwischen, s. entziehen
	embarrassed [im'bærəst]	– verwirrt, verlegen
	engaged [in'geidʒd]	– besetzt, (Telefon)
	enquiry [in'kwaiəri]	– Untersuchung, Befragung
	estate [is'teit]	– hier: Siedlung
	to estimate ['estimeit]	– schätzen
	evidence ['evidəns]	– Beweis(e)
	exceptional(ly) [ik'sepʃnəl]	– außergewöhnlich
	to exchange [iks'tʃeindʒ]	– austauschen
	expense [iks'pens]	– (Un-)Kosten
	experienced [iks'piəriənst]	– erfahren
	extensive [iks'tensiv]	– weitläufig
F	factual ['fæktjuəl]	– sachlich
	failure ['feiljə]	– Mißerfolg
	fence [fens]	– hier: Hehler
	firm(ly) [fe:m]	– fest
	fishy ['fiʃi]	– komisch, verdächtig, „faul“
	flash [flæʃ]	– Blitz
	fog [fɔg]	– (Nebel-) Dunst
	fold [fould]	– Falte
	to forecast ['fɔ:ka:st]	– vorhersagen
	to forge [fɔ:dʒ]	– fälschen
	freezer ['fri:zə]	– Gefrierfach
	to furnish ['fə:niʃ]	– ausstatten, möblieren
	furtive(ly) ['fə:tiv]	– verstohlen, heimlich
	fussy ['fʌsi]	– wählerisch, heikel
G	game [geim]	– Spiel
	to give the ~ away	– jd. verraten
	glance [gla:ns]	– Blick, blicken
	go-between ['goubitwi:n]	– Mittels-, Verbindungsmann
	to go in for	– s. befassen mit, begeistern für
	to grope for [group]	– tasten nach

	to growl [graul]	– knurren, murren
	gruff [grʌf]	– mürrisch, grob
	to grumble [grʌmbl]	– murren, schimpfen
	guilt [gilt]	– Schuld
	to gut [gʌt]	– ausnehmen
H	to hail [heil]	– heranwinken
	handcuffs ['hændkʌfs]	– Handschellen
	harm [haːm]	– Schaden, Unheil
	to harness ['haːnis]	– zäumen
	harsh [haːʃ]	– rauh, scharf
	head office ['hed'ɔfis]	– Zentrale
	headquarters ['hedkwɔːtəz]	– Zentrale; Hauptquartier
	health [helθ]	– Gesundheit; Wohl (-ergehen)
	to hesitate ['heziteit]	– zögern
	hint [hint]	– Hinweis, Hilfe
	to hire ['haiə]	– (ver)mieten
	hiss [his]	– zischen
	without a hitch [hitʃ]	– reibungslos
	hoarse [hɔːs]	– heiser
	hold-up ['houldʌp]	– Stau
	horrified ['hɔrifaid]	– entsetzt
	horseradish ['hɔːsrædiʃ]	– Meerrettich
	hostility [hos'tiliti]	– Feindseligkeit
	to hug [hʌg]	– i. Arm halten
	humbly [hʌmbli]	– demütig
	hunch [hʌntʃ]	– (Vor-)Ahnung
	husky ['hʌski]	– heiser
	to hustle [hʌsl]	– stoßen, drängen
I	identity card [ai'dentiti kaːd]	– Ausweis
	illegal [il'liːgəl]	– ungesetzlich
	impeccable [im'pekəbl]	– untadelig
	incident ['insidənt]	– Vorfall
	incredulous [in'kredjuləs]	– ungläubig
	to indicate ['indikeit]	– hier: ein Zeichen geben

	inquisitive [in'kwizitiv]	– neugierig, fragend
	to insist [in'sist]	– bestehen auf, beharren
	to interrogate [in'terəgeit]	– verhören
	to intervene [intə'viːn]	– einschreiten
	invariably [in'vɛəriəbli]	– unveränderlich, konstant
	investigation [investi'geiʃn]	– Untersuchung
	to involve [in'vɔlv]	– verwickeln, beteiligen
J	(traffic) jam [dʒæm]	– Stau
	jaw [dʒɔː]	– Kiefer
	joint [dʒɔint]	– „Bude", „Laden"
	junk [dʒʌnk]	– Dschunke, chines. Segelschiff
L	landlord ['lænlɔːd]	– (Gast-)Wirt
	layabout ['leiəbaut]	– Gammler
	lifebelt ['laifbelt]	– Rettungsring
	likely ['laikli]	– wahrscheinlich
	liquid ['likwid]	– Flüssigkeit
	literally ['litərəli]	– buchstäblich
	log fire ['lɔgfaiə]	– Kaminfeuer
	to be at a loss [lɔs]	– in Verlegenheit sein
	lumberjack ['lʌmbədʒæk]	– Holzfäller
	lump [lʌmp]	– Klumpen, Kloß, „Frosch"
	(to make) a lunge for [lʌndʒ]	– losstürzen auf
M	manners ['mænəz]	– Benehmen, Manieren
	mastermind ['maːstəmaind]	– Kopf, Chef
	Mediterranean [meditə'reinjən]	– Mittelmeer-, südländisch
	medium ['miːdiəm]	– mittel~
	mischief ['mistʃif]	– Unheil, Unglück
	to misdial ['mis'daiəl]	– falsch wählen (Tel.)
	monk [mʌŋk]	– Mönch
	muffled [mʌfld]	– gedämpft
N	to nag [næg]	– meckern, nörgeln
O	to object [əb'dʒekt]	– einwenden

to occur [ə'kəː] – hier: (über-)kommen
to overawe [ouvər'ɔː] – einschüchtern
to overtake [ouvə'teik] – überholen

P to pace [peis] – schreiten, durchschreiten
particular(ly) [pə'tikjulə] – besonders
to pass [paːs] – hier: in Umlauf bringen
peak [piːk] – Gipfel
to persuade [pə'sweid] – überreden, überzeugen
phial [faiəl] – Fläschchen, Ampulle
to pick [pik] – knacken, öffnen
plump [plʌmp] – mollig
pointed ['pɔintid] – gezielt
pork chop ['pɔːk tʃɔp] – Schweinekotelette
posh [pɔʃ] – pikfein
precious ['preʃəs] – wertvoll
precious stone – Edelstein
precise [pri'sais] – genau
premature(ly) [premə'tjue] – vorzeitig
preoccupied [pri'ɔkjupaid] – beschäftigt, gefangen
to pretend [pri'tend] – vortäuschen
previous ['priːviəs] – vorherig(e)
to produce [prə'djuːs] – (hervor)holen
prospect ['prouspekt] – Vorschau, Aussichten
to prove [pruːv] – beweisen
provisions [prə'viʒnz] – Vorräte
to prowl [praul] – schleichen, s. herumtreiben

R rack [ræk] – Ablage, Brett
raid [reid] – Razzia
ransom ['rænsəm] – Lösegeld
rat [ræt] – Ratte
to smell a ~ – den Braten riechen
ray [rei] – Strahl

to realize ['riəlaiz]	– bemerken, klarwerden
receipt [ri'si:t]	– Quittung
red-handed ['redhændid]	– auf frischer Tat
red herring [red 'heriŋ]	– Ablenkungsmanöver
to register ['redʒistə]	– anmelden, registrieren
to regret [ri'gret]	– bedauern
to reject [ri'dʒekt]	– verwerfen
to rejoice [ri'dʒɔis]	– frohlocken
release [rili:s]	– freilassen
reliable [ri'laiəbl]	– verläßlich
relieved [ri'li:vd]	– erleichtert
to replace [ri'pleis]	– ersetzen, weichen
rickshaw ['rikʃɔ:]	– Rikscha, Handkarren
ring master	– Zirkusdirektor
roadblock ['rəudblɔk]	– Straßensperre
to rock [rɔk]	– schaukeln
rumour ['ru:mə]	– Gerücht
to run dry	– austrocknen
to run out (short) of	– zu Ende gehen, nicht mehr haben
S saveloy ['sævilɔi]	– Zervelatwurst(brot)
scale [skeil]	– Ebene
scoop [sku:p]	– Fang
scorn [skɔ:n]	– Verachtung
scratch [skrætʃ]	– Kratzer
to search [sə:tʃ]	– durchsuchen
sensible ['sensibl]	– vernünftig
sentence ['sentəns]	– hier: Urteil(sspruch)
a shade [ʃeid]	– eine Spur, ein bißchen
to shadow ['ʃædou]	– beschatten, beobachten
shallow ['ʃælou]	– flach, ohne Tiefgang
on shanks's pony ['ʃæŋksiz 'pouni]	– auf Schusters Rappen, zu Fuß
to share [ʃεə]	– teilen
to shatter ['ʃætə]	– zerschmettern

to shiver ['ʃivə]	– zittern, frösteln
to shroud [ʃraud]	– einhüllen, verschleiern
to shrug [ʃrʌg]	– mit der Schulter zucken
to sigh [sai]	– seufzen
significant [si'gnifikənt]	– bedeutsam, auffallend
sinister ['sinistə]	– böse
skidmark ['skidma:k]	– Bremsspur
sleuth [slu:θ]	– Detektiv
to smack [smæk]	– lecken, schmatzen
to sneer [sniə]	– feixen, höhnisch grinsen
soil [sɔil]	– Boden
solution [sə'lu:ʃn]	– Lösung
to solve [sɔlv]	– lösen
to speed [spi:d]	– (zu) schnell fahren
spice [spais]	– Gewürz
squad [skwɔd]	– Abteilung
square… [skwεə]	– Quadrat…
squashed [skwɔʃt]	– plattgedrückt
staff [sta:f]	– Belegschaft
to start [sta:t]	– hier: zusammenfahren, er-, aufschrecken
stock [stɔk]	– Vorrat
stocky ['stɔki]	– stämmig
striking(ly) ['straikiŋ]	– bestechend
subterranean [sʌbtə'reinjən]	– unterirdisch
subtle [sʌtl]	– fein, schlau
supplied [sə'plaid]	– vorrätig, vorhanden
to suspect [səs'pekt]	– vermuten, verdächtigen
suspicion [səs'piʃn]	– Vermutung
suspicious [səs'piʃəs]	– argwöhnisch, verdächtig

to swallow [ˈswɔlou] – schlucken
to sway [swei] – schaukeln
to swear [sweə] – fluchen
sweep [swi:p] – kehren, fegen
to make a clean ~ – reinen Tisch machen
T takings [ˈteikiŋz] – Einnahmen
tankard [ˈtæŋkəd] – Krug
tape [teip] – Tonband
task [ta:sk] – Aufgabe
tasteful [ˈteistful] – geschmackvoll
to be at the end of one's tether [ˈteðə] – am Ende (seiner Kräfte) sein
to thaw [θɔ:] – tauen
thorough [ˈθʌrə] – gründlich
tie [tai] – Schlips
~ pin – ~ nadel
tight [tait] – eng, dicht
to tighten [ˈtaitən] – zusammenziehen
tight-fisted [ˈtaitˈfistid] – knauserig
tip [tip] – Trinkgeld
to tiptoe [ˈtiptəu] – auf Zehenspitzen gehen
to toss [tɔs] – sich hin u. her werfen
trafficking [ˈtræfikiŋ] – Handel
trap [træp] – Falle
to treat [tri:t] – zum Narren halten
trout [traut] – Forelle
to tuck [tʌk] – ziehen, einpacken
in turn [in tə:n] – seinerseits, wiederum
to turn out [tə:n aut] – sich herausstellen
to twitch [twitʃ] – zucken
U umpteenth [ˈʌmti:nθ] – wiederholt(en), x-ten
unconscious [ʌnˈkɔnʃəs] – bewußtlos
unfortunate(ly) [ʌnˈfɔ:tʃnit] – unglücklicherweise
unless [ʌnˈless] – es sei denn
unlikely [ʌnˈlaikli] – unwahrscheinlich
unoccupied [ˈʌnˈɔkjupaid] – unbewohnt

	unruffled ['ʌn'rʌfld]	– gelassen, unerschüttert
V	valuable ['væljuəbl]	– wertvoll; Wertgegenstand
	value ['vælju:]	– Wert
	to vanish ['væniʃ]	– verschwinden
	vigorous(ly) ['vigərəs]	– heftig
	volume ['vɔlju:m]	– Lautstärke
W	warrant ['wɔrənt]	– Vollmacht
	weary ['wiəri]	– müde
	wholesale ['houlseil]	– Großhandels-
	with a will	– mit Lust und Liebe
	wing [wiŋ]	– hier: Kotflügel
	witness ['witnəs]	– Zeuge; beobachten
X	x-ray ['eksrei]	– Röntgenstrahl
Y	to yell [jel]	– brüllen, schreien

RTB Detektiv

RTB 60 ab 10

RTB 208 ab 10

RTB 1536 ab 10

RTB 1754 ab 10

RTB 1761 ab 12

RTB 1784 ab 12

Ravensburger TaschenBücher